7 BIGGEST MISTAKES THAT CAN WRECK YOUR UTAH ACCIDENT CASE

AND HOW TO AVOID THEM

The Utah Accident and Injury Guide

Kenneth L. Christensen
Attorney at Law

Printed in the United States of America.

ISBN: 978-0-615-36653-1

Walubi Graphics
Salt Lake City, Utah
801-662-0667
www.walubigraphics.com

TABLE OF CONTENTS

Why Did I Write This Book?

Since publishing my first book, I have received numerous stories and feedback from people who have had bad experiences with insurance companies after an accident. Many times, the person's own insurance has been guilty of causing the most frustrating problems. Unfortunately for most of these accident victims, they have found themselves in a position where it was too late to file a claim, or they have settled for much less than they should have. Each time the response is, "I wish I had read your book before I was in my accident."

One of the claims I recently handled perfectly demonstrates the vulnerability of Utah accident victims. The case was complex and involved significant loss, a familiar scenario that insurance companies successfully manipulate. In October 2009, a man we will call Rob lost his parents in a rollover car accident while traveling to Seattle to visit family. Rob's mother was ejected from the vehicle and died instantly from her injuries. His father suffered traumatic head injuries in the accident and passed away en route to the local hospital.

Several weeks had passed since the car accident; Rob and his family had completed the funeral services and were mourning the loss of their parents. The insurance company had called several times since the accident, but the family had not been ready to speak with them at the time. Rob did return the insurance company's call, but after expressing condolences, the company's representative told Rob that the family did not have a case, and the case file was being closed.

In addition to the funeral expenses, Rob was left with bills totaling close to $45,000 for the life-flight and the emergency treatment administered to his late father. Rob was at a loss and knew instinctively that his parents' case should not be closed. Fortunately, a friend of Rob's had requested a copy of my book, and after seeing the treatment that Rob was receiving from the insurance company, he gave the book to Rob and suggested he give me a call.

I met with Rob and his family and did a lot of listening. I listened to the family talk endearingly about how their parents had come to America from a communist nation so their children could have a better life, and how they had sacrificed everything for the family. I listened to each of the adult children talk about how their parents' deaths had impacted their relationships with other family members. The insurance company had given Rob and his family the clear message that their parents' lives had no value. Having never dealt with a death in the family, let alone their parents, Rob and his siblings had many questions. We talked about insurance claims and wrongful death actions, and together we outlined a plan of three specific ways I would present the case to the insurance company. I gathered photographs, witness statements, and medical bills. I also met with the insurance adjustor, and in so doing, discovered that his reason for initially denying the claim was incorrect. When I challenged the adjustor on his rationale for denying the claim, he responded by offering a small settlement. Of course, the proposed settlement left Rob and his family in a substantially better position than the initial denial of the claim, but I knew that even this proposed settlement was insufficient.

We eventually settled the case, receiving the maximum amount allowed under three different insurance policies. This settlement came after the insurance company said the family didn't have a case. It felt good to assist Rob and his family, to help when they were clearly not in a position to find justice on their own.

Unfortunately Rob's case is not unusual, and that, in a nutshell, is why I have written this book.

Today, it is more difficult than ever for people to receive honest answers to their questions following an accident. If you have been in an accident, I would certainly like you to contact our firm and allow us to evaluate your claim. You will never be under any obligation to hire us. I have written this book, which is free to Utah residents, because I want you to have this valuable information - whether you hire our firm, another firm, or no attorney at all.

I am tired of insurance companies taking advantage of people before they have a chance to talk to an attorney. For years, one major insurance company encouraged claimants not to hire an attorney. Many of our clients have told us the adjustor advised them not to hire an attorney because "it won't make a difference." That statement is occasionally true, but for the majority of cases, insurance companies mislead accident victims because they know the case is worth much more than they are offering, or what they plan to offer. (This is why insurance adjustors have actually asked me to represent them for their own injury cases!) You may not need an attorney to represent you in your case, but you should at least be armed with this important information right from the beginning of your claim.

I also strongly believe that the information in the following pages will give you a realistic outlook on the value typically associated with accident cases in Utah. My guess is that you, like I, have had enough of outrageous lawyer advertisements where attorneys snap their fingers or wave huge checks making people think personal injury claims are "easy" or part of a "lawsuit lottery." The information in this book will help you find the best lawyer for your case.

I am willing to share the information contained in this book because I do not like to see people accept a bad deal or give up on fighting for their rights simply because they do not know how to proceed. This book outlines what you need to know, and what you must avoid in order to preserve your rights and get what you deserve.

This information is now available to you without any pressure - and without the appointment that most attorneys require you to make in order to receive basic information on accident cases. I hope you will read this book and become informed before you fall victim to those who would take advantage of you at a vulnerable time.

Legal Disclaimer

(You knew it was coming!)

I cannot give legal advice in this book. The suggestions and the warnings I provide in this book are not a substitute for consulting with or hiring an attorney. Please remember that I do not represent you, and I cannot give you legal advice unless and until you hire me and I have agreed in writing to accept your case.

Part I Understanding Your Personal Injury Case

Myths:

The most common misconceptions about personal injury cases are:

- If you write the insurance company a nice, reasonable letter, you will receive a reasonable settlement offer.
- If you are in an accident, you always need an attorney.
- When you are in an accident and the insurance company asks you to give a recorded statement, you have to give them the statement, or they won't settle with you.
- You can't get a rental car unless you give a recorded statement to the insurance adjustor.
- The insurance company for the person who hit you is obligated to pay your medical bills as they become due.
- If you are injured in an accident, and it was not your fault, there will always be an insurance company that will pay for your injuries, pain and suffering, and lost wages.
- The insurance adjustor is being nice now; once I ask for a settlement he'll continue to be nice.
- Insurance adjustors will only obtain the medical records relating to my accident if I sign their authorization form.
- Utah juries are generous.

What is a Personal Injury Case?

A personal injury or wrongful death case is any type of claim where a person has been injured or killed due to someone else's negligence. If you are in an automobile accident, and the only thing damaged is your car, you may have a property damage claim, but not a personal injury claim. Our firm does not handle cases with only property damage, but there are attorneys who handle these types of claims. We focus on accidents where there are serious physical injuries involved. If you are in an automobile accident, and both you and your car are damaged, you may have both a property damage claim and a personal injury claim.

If a person is killed by the negligence of another, their surviving family members may have a wrongful death claim against the other party. The law of each state or jurisdiction differs significantly regarding what can be recovered in a wrongful death case. If you have specific questions about a wrongful death claim, please feel free to contact my office, and I will be happy to discuss them with you. My contact information can be found in the back of this book. Additionally, my business partner and I have authored the *Utah Wrongful Death Book.* We offer this book free of charge so family members can discuss important issues and make decisions together in the comfort of their homes before ever speaking with the insurance companies or hiring an attorney.

How Do Insurance Companies and Adjustors Operate?

After an accident, all parties involved should contact their insurance companies. In Utah, the insurance company for the car in which you were riding will typically cover your initial $3,000 in medical bills (this is known as PIP or No-Fault Coverage). The at-fault driver's insurance company is responsible for property damage, reimbursing your insurance company for your PIP claim, and your bodily injury claim. The bodily injury claim can include past and future medical bills, lost wages, future loss of earning capacity, loss of enjoyment of life, and pain and suffering.

Understand that insurance adjustors have no obligation to inform you of your rights. Insurance adjustors are trained to take advantage of the lack of knowledge most claimants have about the legal system and the value of their accident claim. The adjustor on your case may seem like a nice person who is friendly and pleasant over the phone, and even concerned with your welfare. In fact, he or she might actually be a nice person. However, never forget that insurance adjustors' primary job is to protect the insurance company. The way they protect the insurance company is by finding a way to not give you any money. If they have to pay you money, they try to pay as little as possible in order to resolve the matter and make it go away.

What Must Be Proven to Win Your Case?

Some people contact our office with the misconception that they should be compensated just because someone else was careless or negligent. A personal injury claim requires two things: first, someone else was careless or negligent; and second, the other person's carelessness caused you harm. Unless someone else's carelessness caused your injuries, you do not have a viable case.

You must also understand that in Utah, the law of comparative negligence controls how much money, if any, you can recover from someone who causes your injury. If the jury finds that you were partially at fault in the accident, they will reduce the amount of money you recover by the amount you were at fault. If the jury finds you were more than half at fault for your injuries, you will recover nothing.

For example, if your damages total $100,000, and if a jury awards you that amount but determines that you were 20% at fault, your $100,000 would be reduced by 20%, or $20,000, leaving you with $80,000. If the jury finds that you were 51% or more at fault in your accident, you will recover nothing. It may not seem fair, but it is the law in Utah. After we evaluate your case, we will discuss with you the issue of comparative negligence to determine whether or not you have a case worth pursuing.

Do You Really Need an Attorney to Handle Your Case?

You definitely do not need an attorney for every injury case. For example, if your automobile case involves little or no property damage and/or your injuries are minor, it can be handled on your own by utilizing the information provided in this book. If you were to hire an attorney in these smaller cases the fees and costs might leave little or nothing for you after medical bills are paid, which would not be fair to you. Of course, there are many factors to consider when deciding whether you should hire an attorney. We offer free consultations to help you make the right decision for your case.

What Are the Benefits of Hiring an Attorney?

Over the last two decades, billion-dollar insurance companies have used their public relations machines to create a perception that lawsuits are frivolous and unnecessary. This is false and misleading, but over time their propaganda has had a tremendous effect on juries and their verdicts. This is called tort reform. The success that insurance companies have had in tainting the minds of jurors has emboldened them to low-ball injured victims.

Insurance companies have made their fortunes by taking advantage of individuals who are inexperienced with the insurance claims process. Today, injured victims must educate themselves regarding the claims process, their rights, and the insurance companies' obligations if they want to have any hope of receiving a fair settlement. In many cases, the best result will be achieved by hiring an attorney who specializes in this area to help you navigate through the claims process.

As explained earlier, not every case requires an attorney. That being said, personally handling an insurance claim – especially when you are trying to heal from serious injuries – can be one of the most confusing, time-consuming and stressful things you have ever done. Not only will a good personal injury lawyer deal with the insurance company so you can focus on getting the medical care you need, but he/she will also get a better settlement for you than trying to do it yourself. A recent study by the Insurance Research Council confirms this fact, finding that injury victims with an attorney receive three and a half times more than people without legal representation.

Another benefit to hiring a personal injury attorney is the manner in which he/she is paid. Most lawyers charge by the hour or require their clients to pay an up-front fee for their services. This type of fee structure can be a financial impossibility for injury victims, many of whom are facing mounting medical bills and are unable to work because of their injuries. Fortunately, most personal injury attorneys work on a contingency fee basis, meaning that they will never charge for their services until they win or settle the case. If the case is successful, you pay them a percentage of your recovery. If the case is unsuccessful, however, you will not be responsible for their efforts.

Who Will Pay My Medical Bills After The Accident?

Every car insurance policy is required to have Personal Injury Protection (PIP). This portion of the insurance policy has a minimum of $3,000 available for medical treatment for each person involved in an accident. This coverage is provided by your insurance company. This means your own car insurance company will pay for some of your medical bills even though you didn't cause the accident. This will not affect your insurance rates, because you didn't cause the accident, and after your insurance company has exhausted the $3,000 medical coverage, they will be reimbursed by the insurance company of the driver who caused the accident.

Unfortunately, most PIP coverage only allows for $3,000 in medical bills, but you can have higher limits, so occasionally we will see a policy with $5,000 or even $10,000 in PIP coverage.

What Happens After My PIP Coverage Is Exhausted?

As it pertains to your injury case, the at-fault driver's insurance company will not make payments "along the way" for the medical bills and other expenses incurred. Instead, at the time of settlement, the insurance company will pay you one settlement check for all your damages and losses. What this means is that you – the accident victim – have to find a way to cover payment of those medical expenses until your case settles. It can be extremely frustrating having to pay for unwanted expenses after an accident ... particularly when the accident wasn't your fault! But there are some options available to you:

1. Health Insurance:

If you have health insurance coverage, it is best to have the medical provider forward your bills to the health insurance company for payment.

a. Pros: Even though the medical bills are accident related, the health insurance company will pay the bills and keep them from being sent to a collection company and affecting your credit.

b. Cons: Some policies require payment of co-pays, deductibles and often only cover 80% of the medical expenses, leaving you responsible for the other 20%. You may have to pay these co-pays and deductibles to ensure they are not sent to collections. However, you are entitled to reimbursement at the time of settlement for every expense paid out-of-pocket.

2. Set Up A Lien With The Medical Provider:

A lien is an agreement that is often available in cases where an attorney represents you for your injuries. It is a written binding agreement between the client, medical provider, and attorney, and specifically indicates that the medical provider will wait for payment until the case settles. The attorney agrees to pay the medical provider before releasing any settlement funds to the client, and the client agrees that no matter the outcome of the case, the bills will eventually be paid by the client.

a. Pros: If your attorney is able to set up a lien with your medical providers, you will not have to worry about paying the medical bills until your case settles.

b. Cons: Some medical providers refuse to accept liens or wait for payment until the time of settlement.

3. Pay Cash/Monthly Payments:

a. Pros: If you pay all of your medical expenses up front with cash, you can typically receive a cash payment discount. If you are unable to pay the whole bill at once, but instead make minimum monthly payments, you can keep the account current and avoid having the account sent to collections and affecting your credit.

b. Cons: Not everyone has the ability to pay cash for unanticipated medical expenses.

4. Let The Bill Go To Collections And Then Try And Set Up A Lien With The Collection Company:

a. Pros: Even if the medical provider will not accept a lien, some collection companies will do so.

b. Cons: Some collection companies that accept liens will still record the overdue payment on your credit report.

I recognize that none of the options above are very attractive, particularly for those who don't have health insurance. Just remember that the at-fault insurance company doesn't get off the hook – they are responsible for all accident-related treatment at the time of settlement, and you'll be entitled to reimbursement of all your out-of-pocket expenses at that time.

Do I Ever Have to Pay Back the Medical Bills That Were Paid by My Own Health Insurance Company?

Believe it or not, the answer is often yes. There are state and federal laws that may require you to reimburse your own health insurance company or your employer's health plan from any money you recover in your personal injury case. It is important that you review with your attorney the terms of your own insurance policy to see if you're required to repay any of these costs. Your insurance company's right to be reimbursed for medical bills from your settlement or verdict is known as "subrogation." This is a complicated area of the law. You should discuss this issue with your attorney as soon as possible after your accident.

At Christensen & Hymas, we are generally successful in reducing the health insurance company's subrogation claim, which we give back to you as our client. For example, if you have $15,000 in medical expenses paid by your health insurance plan, we can often negotiate with your health insurance company to accept a reduced amount of $10,000 as payment in full. The additional $5,000 goes to you.

Part II
The 7 Biggest Mistakes That Can Wreck Your Utah Accident Case

Over the years I have compiled what I consider to be the 7 biggest mistakes that can wreck your accident case. These mistakes are based on my experience with accident cases and discussions with judges and jurors after trials.

This information helps level the playing field between accident victims and the insurance companies. My hope is that Utah residents are able to read this book before they ever get in an accident, or at least before they make any of the mistakes enumerated below. Avoiding these pitfalls will keep the insurance company from taking advantage of people who are inexperienced with the claims process and the common tactics insurance companies employ to protect their bottom line.

Mistake #1

Allowing The Insurance Company To Make You Feel Guilty For Bringing A Claim

Almost every person who comes to my office seeking answers to their legal questions indicates, almost in a guilty voice, that he or she is not the type to sue. I understand that no one wants to sue another person or be involved in litigation. But what you need to realize is that the insurance industry, in an attempt to keep its profit margins high, makes people feel guilty for bringing a claim – and even worse, for hiring a lawyer to protect their interests! They want you to believe that all personal injury claims are frivolous, and that anyone who files a lawsuit after an accident is doing so because he or she is a greedy person. This couldn't be farther from the truth. The individuals I have helped over the years are honest, hard-working people with legitimate claims who simply need help recovering what they've lost after an accident. If this was not true, why would close to 90% of all personal injury claims in Utah be settled by the insurance companies without ever having to file a lawsuit?

This is insurance company propaganda at its best, and an attempt by the insurance industry to protect its profits by persuading accident victims to accept quick or small settlements. I am proud of all my past and present clients, who have recognized these deceitful tactics for what they are, and have decided to stand up to the insurance companies and force them to treat injured people fairly.

The innocent victim who defends himself from being taken advantage of, who fights to be fairly compensated, or who seeks the advice of an attorney is not greedy. Often times, it is just the opposite. The people willing to seek counsel and protect themselves from injustice are more often the people who end up getting fair compensation. Getting what is owed under the law is not greed. The party who refuses to pay what they owe, on the other hand, squarely falls into the greed category, in my opinion.

Utah is full of peaceful, kind, non-confrontational people (one of the many reasons I chose to raise my family here). But when an insurance adjustor tries to convince you to drop a claim or accept less than a fair amount, don't give up! By refusing to give in, you protect not only your own rights, but those of your family members, friends, neighbors, and members of your community. When insurance companies are not held accountable, it encourages still more dangerous behavior at the expense of the community's financial resources and safety.

Mistake #2

Believing That The Insurance Company Is Your Friend And Will Treat You Fairly

I can't tell you how many stories I have heard over the years from frustrated people who realized they accepted a very unfair settlement offer from the insurance company. Their explanations often have a familiar theme. "The adjustor seemed so nice. He told me they would take care of me." "She was so pleasant and seemed concerned about my injuries. I thought she was on my side."

These individuals have failed to realize that insurance adjustors are trained to take advantage of the lack of knowledge most people have about their legal rights and the value of their claims. The adjustor assigned to your claim may seem like a nice person – in fact, he or she might be a nice person – but never forget that the adjustor's primary job is to protect the insurance company. The way they do this is by either finding a way not to pay you at all, or to pay you as little as possible in order to resolve the matter. Their job, their pay, and their promotions depend on the extent to which they make money for the insurance company. They are not compensated or rewarded for giving their company's money to claimants. Many clients have told me that they believed their own insurance company would take care of them because of the good relationship they had with the agent who sold them the policy. What they don't understand is that when an injury occurs, the claims department handles the claim – not the agent who sold them the policy. The job of the claims adjustor is to minimize or avoid the obligation to pay you. Adjustors do not care about your relationship with the insurance agent. They don't care that you've been a customer of the insurance company for 25 years and never had an accident or filed a claim. Nor does it matter to them that you've never been late in paying a premium. Adjustors are instructed to resolve the claim for as little as possible. If they can settle the claim for fifty cents on the dollar, they will not hesitate to do so, no matter what you think is fair or reasonable.

Below are some examples of seemingly kind and helpful gestures from insurance adjustors which often have a much more self-serving purpose:

• *"I want to help you get a rental car. But first, I need a recorded statement from you to process the claim."* An adjustor may, in fact, need some information from you to investigate a claim and make proper payments on the claim (such as providing a rental car to you). But you are not required to give the insurance company a recorded statement, which is later transcribed and often used against you. A simple example of this can be seen at the beginning of a recorded statement, when the adjustor asks the injured person, *"How are you doing?"* and the person responds, *"Fine, thanks."* A normal response for a question that you're probably asked several times a day, right? But I've seen instances where the insurance company has later questioned whether an individual was really injured in an accident because apparently they were doing *"fine"* at the time the recorded statement was taken. (A better response to this question would have been, *"I'm OK, considering ... ."*) It seems ridiculous, but this is often the type of nonsense that an honest, well-meaning victim can encounter by simply allowing a statement to be recorded.

• *"In order to pay your claim, I'll need your medical bills and records. You've got enough on your plate right now. I'm happy to get them for you if you just sign a medical release."* Watch out for an offer like this. I never allow my clients to sign an adjustor's release for documents or authorization for information-gathering. These documents are almost always crafted to grant the adjustor permission to retrieve virtually every file from your past. This means the adjustor can access every medical record, regardless of whether it has anything to do with your accident. He or she can acquire every one of your school and employment records, your personal files, and any other piece of written information about you. Your entire life can be scrutinized without restriction. If the adjustor makes such a request, he or she is likely looking for two things: 1) medical records that show any prior injury to the parts of your body injured in the accident, so that the insurance company can argue that the pre-existing condition is to blame for your current symptoms ... even if the prior injury was years ago; and/or 2) records that can be used to discredit you or put you in a bad light, such as psychological records or medical records that may be embarrassing to you and provide the insurance company with leverage so that you will offer little or no resistance in accepting the company's proposed settlement offer.

• *"Let me give you a piece of friendly advice. Don't hire a lawyer. The attorney will just take the settlement money that's rightfully yours.*" As I noted earlier, studies show that this statement is completely false - injured people with an attorney receive significantly more than those without legal counsel. In fact, the Utah legislature has now passed a specific law prohibiting insurance companies from making these types of statements! Despite this law, there are still claims adjustors who discourage people from hiring an attorney. They know that with an experienced attorney on hand, they will have to pay more for the claim than they originally wanted.

Mistake #3

Not Seeking Immediate Medical Care Or Cooperating Fully With Your Doctor

One of the most critical parts of your case is how you feel and how your injuries affect your ability to function on a daily basis. Your doctor is required to keep accurate and detailed records of your medical history and care. The insurance companies will base the value of your case on your doctor's medical conclusions and the critical information in your medical records. Don't let the doctor guess how you are feeling. Tell the medical providers exactly how your discomfort is affecting you every time you see them. A single notation from a doctor can change the insurance company's evaluation of a claim. The assumption by most people (therefore, most jurors) is that the medical records will be accurate. Since accident victims are required to prove that they were injured in the accident, the trust placed in those medical records becomes central to the process. If there are errors in the records, you must talk further with your doctor and request additional documentation.

Not only is it important to tell your doctor everything that hurts, it is equally important to be honest with the doctor about treatment and injuries prior to your accident. Your doctor will ask about your prior condition and base his medical opinions on the information you provide him. Once a lawsuit is filed, the insurance companies will obtain your prior medical records and if they are inconsistent with the history given to your doctor, it will ruin your credibility and your case.

It is also crucial to follow your doctor's orders. If your doctor tells you to get therapy three times a week, but you only go once, you will damage your case. I once had a mother of four young boys come into my office with a neck injury following an automobile accident. Her doctor recommended physical therapy several times a week but, like many young mothers, she pushed her treatment to the side so she could focus on her children. She hoped her injuries would get better over time. After four months and no sign of improvement, she finally started physical therapy.

In a sense, her actions are admirable. She tried to move on with her life, not make a big deal about her injuries. She tried to do whatever she could do, tough it out, and hoped she would get better. But what do you think the insurance company did with this information? Believe it or not, the insurance company hired a doctor who was willing to testify that my client must have injured her neck while caring for her young children instead of in her car accident!

Did the insurance company win? No! We were able to fight for her and get a good result, although it took much longer than it would have had she followed her doctor's orders. These arguments are repeatedly made by insurance adjustors to avoid a fair settlement. The bottom line is when you are injured in an accident, you must follow the advice of your doctor and follow up with referrals, or risk something less than a fair resolution of your claim. Even if you have to cancel an appointment or two, you should make sure there are no significant gaps in time during the course of your medical treatment.

Mistake #4

Hiding Past Accidents And Injuries From Your Attorney

Once you begin a case, the opposing side is allowed to explore your past accident history to determine whether your injuries and condition could have been caused by another accident. This should be obvious, but you need to be up front and honest with your attorney about any injuries or accidents that occurred before or after the current accident. Usually the insurance company, its adjustors, and attorneys already have substantial information about your prior accidents. The entire insurance industry maintains an extensive database of people who have been in prior accidents and asserted claims. If you try to hide a prior accident history, either from your attorney or the insurance company, it can severely damage your case, if not destroy it.

The same is true for prior injuries and medical care. If you saw a doctor before the accident you can bet there is a written record (i.e., chart note) that the insurance company will find. Do not hide anything. Do not decide what you think your attorney should know. If your attorney knows about your prior medical history in the beginning, then he or she can do something about it or at least manage the case in an appropriate way to minimize its damaging effects on your current case. But if you hide this information and your attorney finds out later, you will either lose your case or receive substantially less.

The value of a case rests largely upon an accident victim's ability to demonstrate – in a convincing manner – the extent to which the accident has affected his or her life. Credibility is the key! Do not jeopardize your case by failing to disclose everything. All I ask of a client is this: Tell me the truth, the whole truth… and let me make the best of it.

Mistake #5

Misrepresenting Your Activity Level

To be successful in a personal injury claim, you need to be totally honest. This is particularly true in today's climate, where many jurors are suspicious of personal injury plaintiffs to begin with. When I wrote the first edition of this book, I explained how accident victims should be aware of insurance companies hiring private investigators to conduct videotape surveillance. If someone claims he cannot run, climb, or stoop, and then is caught doing so on videotape, he can forget about his claim. There is no explanation (other than "you got my brother, not me. See that tattoo?") that can overcome the eye of the camera. This warning still holds true today, but with the proliferation of social media websites over the past decade, insurance companies rarely need to hire private investigators to conduct video surveillance anymore.

Social media gives them endless opportunities to take innocuous comments, photos, or videos out of context in an attempt to minimize a claim's value. Insurance companies, adjustors, and their attorneys are checking Facebook, Twitter, and looking at blogs to get information about you, the accident victim. There may be valuable information about you on these sites that could severely damage your personal injury claim.

Why are insurance companies looking at social media sites?

- To confirm or disprove the severity of your injury.
- To confirm or disprove your ability to perform activities and sports.
- To confirm or disprove your ability to work.
- To confirm or disprove whether you interact normally with friends and family.

Pictures, videos, personal information, posts and comments can wreck your case. You must be aware of how your pictures and comments will be viewed. Sometimes even the most innocent and seemingly irrelevant things can be twisted to make it look as if you were not injured or that you are lying about being injured. Even making the pages private may not stop the insurance company from seeing it. You may inadvertently make a friend or follower out of someone the adjustor knows, or if your case goes to court, the judge may order you to produce your social media pages.

Here are some tips in dealing with social media:

- Don't post anything that you wouldn't feel comfortable having the insurance adjustor read.
- Check your privacy settings and block anyone you do not know from viewing your personal pages.

- Search your name on all sites that you are a member of and on Google to see what comes up. See what photos you have been tagged in and take the appropriate action to remove photos you are not comfortable with.
- Do not accept any friend requests from people you don't know.

Although these sites are fun and useful tools to keep in touch with friends and family, they can be used against you in many different ways. The bottom line … use common sense and protect yourself as you use your social media websites.

Mistake #6

Waiting Too Long To Seek Legal Help

Too many people have told me they wished they had acted sooner before important deadlines had passed or witnesses had moved or could no longer be found. Almost every kind of action that can be brought has a deadline which prevents someone from bringing that claim after a certain period of time. This is known as the "statute of limitations." There is a statute of limitations on every personal injury action. It is a tool to force plaintiffs to either settle their case or file a lawsuit by a certain date. The goal is a necessary one, to prevent someone from suing a defendant 25 years after a crash that should have been handled within 2 years. The limitation allows defendants to move forward without worrying that they will be sued many years later, and increases the likelihood that witnesses and evidence will still be available.

Your deadline can be affected by the details of your particular case. The statute of limitations for personal injury cases in Utah is typically 4 years from the date of the accident, but it is significantly sooner for wrongful death, medical malpractice, and uninsured and underinsured motorist claims. If your claim involves any type of governmental entity (city, county, state, national) there are specific notice and filing deadlines within 12 months with which you must comply. Understand here, we're not just talking about disputed cases. Even when the government admits it is at fault, the proper paperwork must be filed in less than 12 months. Even when everybody agrees the injury was severe, or the government admits it caused the death of an innocent person through its own neglect, the proper paperwork must be filed in less than 12 months. The reality is that a statute of limitations works to the benefit of the defendants, and against the average person who becomes a victim of another's reckless actions. Do not rely upon the insurance adjustor to give you the statute of limitations deadline for your specific case. Most are unaware of the different deadline requirements. Therefore, it is crucial that you contact an attorney as soon as possible to avoid missing your statute of limitations. Do not wait until the eleventh hour! If you walk into an attorney's office one month before the statute of limitations is going to run out on a serious injury case, you may not be able to find an attorney who is willing to accept the risk of understanding the case and getting the lawsuit filed before the time limit is up. There are just too many "i"s to be dotted and "t"s to be crossed in that little amount of time.

Remember, filing a claim with the insurance company is not the same as filing a lawsuit. If you have not filed a lawsuit within the statute of limitations, you will lose your right to settle your claim. Statute of limitations must be considered and applied on a case by case basis. It is vital that you understand that the statute of limitations requires you to file an actual lawsuit with the court to preserve your case.

Mistake #7

Rushing To Settle Your Case

I have met with many accident victims who, shortly after an accident, express a desire to resolve their insurance claim as quickly as possible. This is certainly understandable - an accident can be an unpleasant memory for anyone (to put it mildly), and most want to wrap up a claim as quickly as possible and move on with their lives! But doing so can have disastrous consequences.

The fact is that many injuries or losses that you've suffered may not become evident until several months after your accident. Insurance adjustors are well aware that, early on, the full extent of an injury is not likely to be known, especially if it's a serious accident. This means that the sooner he or she settles with you, the less the insurance company will have to compensate you for your losses.

Because insurance companies know that a quick settlement is almost always to their benefit - and your detriment - they are happy to agree to it. In fact, one insurance company has begun to send adjustors out to the homes of accident victims just days after an accident. They wave a check for a few hundred dollars in front of the individual, encouraging them to settle the insurance claim on the spot - many times before the accident victim has even seen a doctor!

Whatever else you do, take the time to get a complete and thorough medical diagnosis of your injuries. Even if you receive emergency care, you should have a follow-up with a doctor. Make sure that you've given your injuries plenty of time to manifest themselves fully. It is only at that point that you will be able to determine the fair compensation for your injuries.

Why is it so crucial not to rush to a quick settlement? The answer is simple – you only have"one bite at the apple" when it comes to an automobile insurance claim. There are long-term consequences to making hasty decision, because once you accept payment from the at-fault insurance company, you cannot renegotiate the settlement – regardless of the lasting effects of your injuries. It does not matter if you become incapacitated, or if your family loses you prematurely. The moment you settle your claim, you and your family are responsible for any further expenses you might incur down the road relating to your accident.

I once represented a woman whom I'll call Gretchen. Gretchen came to me a few weeks after a rear-end accident. Her neck was very sore, and she had been diagnosed with "whiplash" injuries by her chiropractor. The at-fault insurance company had stopped by her home a few days before and apologized for her injuries, offering her $500 to settle her claim. Gretchen didn't feel comfortable taking the settlement while she was still in pain, so she came to me for advice.

I told Gretchen that it was in her best interest to wait and see how she healed. That way, she would know the full extent of her injuries and have a clearer view on how she should proceed. At the time, she didn't see the whiplash injuries as a big deal, but thankfully, she heeded the advice.

A few months after that initial visit, Gretchen's whiplash injuries had not resolved – in fact, they had gotten worse. Her chiropractor had referred her to a specialist, who found multiple disc herniations in her cervical spine. He recommended that she undergo an anterior cervical discectomy and fusion (ACDF) – a neck fusion, in laymen's terms. Needless to say, it was a very expensive operation and dramatically affected her life, as well as the value of her insurance claim.

Fortunately, I was able to obtain a substantial settlement that covered all of Gretchen's medical expenses and compensated her for the months of pain, difficulty sleeping, and limited activities with her family that she had to endure after the accident. But the only reason I was able to help her obtain this settlement was because she had waited patiently before pursuing settlement of her claim. That decision made all the difference in terms of her ability to obtain a fair settlement versus the $500 the insurance company had initially offered.

I hope Gretchen's experience serves as a warning flag for you. You have to resist the impulse to rush things after an accident – or to be rushed by an adjustor who knows that you want to get the claim resolved as soon as possible. Your main focus should be to obtain fair and just compensation for your injuries and losses – nothing is more important than that!

Part III
Property Damage Claims

Working with insurance companies after a car accident can be a complicated and frustrating process. When a car is badly damaged, many insurance adjustors will consider it a "total loss" and begin the settlement process. Often times, adjustors will try to settle on a replacement vehicle that the accident victim feels is an unfair substitute. If your car is damaged, but repairable, you have certain rights and privileges the adjustor might fail to mention.

If you have been in an accident and are working with the insurance company, it is important to have proper knowledge of the situation to avoid an unfair settlement. The following tips could help ensure you receive a proper settlement:

1. Insurance papers can be extremely technical and confusing. Before you sign any papers, make sure you fully understand the substance of the agreement. Research terminology or phrases that you do not understand. Also, do not be afraid to contact your insurance company and ask any questions you may have pertaining to the documents they want you to sign. If you sign the papers too soon, you may jeopardize your chances of receiving a fair property damage settlement.

2. If your car is no longer drivable after the accident, your insurance company or the at-fault driver's insurance company can provide you with a rental car. (We recommend against purchasing the rental company's car insurance coverage. Most insurance companies will not pay for this additional coverage). The insurance company may try to put you in a smaller rental car in an attempt to save money. However, they are obligated to provide a rental car that is the same size as the vehicle you were driving at the time of the accident. In addition, if you do not use a rental car for a period of time after the accident, you may be entitled to monetary compensation from the insurance company ranging from $15 to $25 dollars for each day you went without a rental car.

3. Research the value of your car at the time of the accident using your local classifieds or websites such as ksl.com or autotrader.com. Insurance companies tend to value your car by finding similar vehicles as close to your home as possible. It is important that you take the time to properly research the value of your vehicle at the time of the accident. Browse the internet and contact local auto dealers to compare the year, make, model, and condition of your vehicle with other cars on the market. The insurance company will give greatest weight to the vehicles that are closest to the city in which you live. You are not required to accept the adjustor's first settlement offer, especially if you think it is less valuable than your previous vehicle. If this happens, simply counter-offer with vehicles you have found in your own research. You can also ask the insurance company to provide documentation with details on how they valued the vehicle. Do not hesitate to request this information, as the insurance company is obligated to provide this information under Utah State law. The law states that an insurance company must provide documentation for low offers that deviate from the market price of the original vehicle. By obtaining this information, you will also be able to ensure that the adjustor gave you credit for every upgrade or after-market feature in your vehicle.

4. Do not keep the rental car longer than the insurance company permits. You will be held responsible for additional charges. The insurance company will provide a rental vehicle from the date of the accident until they make a reasonable offer for your replacement car. Return the rental the moment the adjustor tells you to do so, even if your settlement check has not arrived.

5. Know your rights. Utah State law provides detailed rules and guidelines by which insurance companies must abide when handling property damage claims. These rules, established in the Utah Administrative Code, can provide you with necessary support as you work with the adjustor. The Code specifies which driver's insurance company must provide a settlement, how the insurance company must value the property damage claim, and what rights you have to defend your claim. These rules are available to the public at www.rules.utah.gov/publicat/code/r590r590-190.htm.

6. Should I have my own insurance company handle the property damage? Even though the accident was not your fault, your own insurance company may offer to handle the property damage claim. This has pros and cons. Typically your own insurance company can handle the claim much faster than the at-fault driver's insurance company. While the at-fault driver's insurance company will not provide you with a rental car or work on the body damage until they've spoken with their insured or obtained a copy of the full police report, your own insurance company is able to move forward without this information. However, your own insurance company may require you to pay your deductible when you pick up your car. This can be hard for some people while trying to pay for medical treatment after the accident. Rest assured that once the at-fault driver's insurance company accepts responsibility for the accident, they will reimburse your insurance company for the property damage claim and your deductible will be returned.

The at-fault driver's insurance company is required by Utah law to provide you with a rental car from the date of the accident until the car has been repaired, or until a fair settlement offer has been made for the replacement of a totaled vehicle. However, if you choose to have your own insurance company handle the property damage claim, you can only receive a rental car for the amount permitted in your insurance contract. If your contract only allows for 20 days of rental car coverage and it takes 30 days to repair the car, you will be responsible for the extra 10 days in rental fees.

7. What can I do when the insurance company wants to repair my vehicle with used parts? If your car was not new at the time of the accident, the insurance company has a right to repair the vehicle with used parts. However, the used parts must be comparable in quality and age. Even though the part is used, the repair shop will use a part from the same manufacturer, the same year, and of the same quality as the original part. Used parts come from a nationally based locating system and can arrive in 1-2 business days. On the other hand, new parts come from the manufacturer or dealerships and typically take weeks before they can be delivered.

8. Many times throughout the repair process, the body shop will discover additional damage that was not initially approved by the insurance company. When this happens the body shop will document the additional damage by taking photographs or asking the insurance adjustor to come to the body shop and inspect the damage. Unless the insurance company can prove that the additional damage is not accident-related, they will be obligated to repair it. If the insurance company refuses to repair the additional damage, you should take the car to other body shops and have them document in writing their opinion that the additional damage must be accident-related because it is not the type of damage that is normally caused by regular wear and tear.

9. If you are unhappy with the repair work done on the vehicle, it is best to return to the original body shop and explain why you are unhappy. Most body shops will do everything in their power to make the customer happy. If the body shop refuses to address your concerns, take the vehicle to other local body shops and have them document what should have been done by the shop. You can then provide the insurance company with this information.

10. Finally, many people wonder if they can take the property damage claim to small claims court. While this may be an option, be extremely careful and consult with an attorney before pursuing this course of action, as it has the potential to completely wipe out your ability to make an injury claim if you were hurt in the accident!

Part IV
The Legal Process
Fewer Cases . . . More Time For You

We are "different."

At Christensen & Hymas, we do not rely on a high volume of cases, and we don't handle every type of case. Each year, we accept a limited number of injury cases from the hundreds of people who ask us to represent them. We do not operate a "high volume, take anything that comes through the door" type of personal injury practice. Instead, we give personal attention to the few cases we do accept. My business partner and I personally handle your case. I do not allow paralegals and assistants to negotiate with the insurance company. My partner and I personally negotiate with the adjustors and attorneys, and we try the cases that go to court. Fewer cases means more time for you and, we believe, better results overall.

I founded Christensen & Hymas because I believe Utah residents deserve more than what most law firms offer. If we accept your case, we will aggressively represent you, keep you up to date on what is happening in your case, and achieve the best possible outcome.

Just because you have been in an accident does not always mean you need an attorney. If we believe you are better off handling the case yourself, we will tell you so. In addition, if we believe you have a claim you cannot win, we will tell you that as well. But, if your case meets our criteria and we accept it, you can rest assured that you will receive our personal attention. You will become part of our law firm family and together as a team, we will decide on the best tactics for your case.

How Do We Handle Personal Injury Cases at Christensen & Hymas?

While every case is different, and not all cases require each of the steps outlined below, the following is a list of what we normally do at our firm when preparing your personal injury claim:

- Evaluate the client's claim during an initial interview, educate the client regarding the legal process for personal injury cases, and determine any deadlines that apply.
- Contact the insurance companies, giving them notice of the claim and asking them to communicate with our office and not the client. This ensures our clients can focus on healing.
- Gather documentary evidence including police accident reports, medical records and bills.
- Analyze the client's insurance policy to see whether there is any coverage the client has that may pay all or a portion of the medical bills while the claim is pending.
- Review the client's insurance policy with the client and make suggestions as to what coverage should be purchased for future protection.
- Interview known witnesses.

- Collect other evidence, such as photographs of the scene of the accident and any property damage involved.
- Analyze the legal issues related to the case, including comparative negligence and any damage limits that may apply.
- Review the medical records and talk to the client's physicians or obtain written reports from them to fully understand the client's condition and any ongoing needs.
- Identify whether the client's health insurance has paid any medical expenses related to the injury claim. If so, ascertain whether any settlement proceeds must be used to reimburse the health insurance plan.
- Prepare a demand package to be sent to the insurance company in an attempt to settle the case.
- Negotiate a fair settlement. At Christensen & Hymas, we are able to successfully settle 90% of our cases without ever having to sue the person who caused the accident.
- If the insurance company is unwilling to make a reasonable settlement offer, discuss the benefits of filing a lawsuit with the client.
- If suit is filed, prepare the client, witnesses, and healthcare providers for depositions.
- Prepare written questions and answers and take the deposition of the defendant and other witnesses.
- Prepare for and attend mediation for potential settlement before trial.

- Go to court to set a trial date.
- Prepare for trial and/or settlement before trial.
- Prepare the client and witnesses for trial.
- Prepare medical and demonstrative exhibits for trial.
- File briefs and motions with the court to eliminate surprises at trial.
- Take the case to trial with a jury or judge.
- Analyze the jury's verdict to determine if either side has good grounds to appeal the case.

How Much Is My Case Worth?

This is a question we often hear from clients in our initial interview. We tell our clients that every case is different, and it is impossible to know the value of a case until we have collected all the facts. Beware of attorneys who tell you your case is worth $XXX,XXX before knowing all the facts in an effort to have you sign a fee agreement. It is a dangerous, unreliable practice and can cause problems when it is time to settle your case. Once we have gathered all the facts, conducted discovery, spoken with your doctors, and prepared a demand package, then we will be able to discuss the value of your case.

Why You Should Hire Christensen & Hymas?

There are many attorneys who advertise for personal injury cases. Unfortunately, some of these attorneys have so many small cases in their offices that no case gets their personal attention. Others have no real intention of trying your case themselves, and if the case cannot be settled with the insurance company, they will refer the case to a new attorney for trial. There are good, experienced attorneys in this field, but it can be very difficult for a consumer to separate the good from the bad.

As I mentioned earlier, "we are different." Rather than run around trying to manage hundreds of cases, we carefully select the cases we will accept at any one time. Being selective of the cases we take requires us to decline numerous cases each year; however, it also ensures that the clients and cases we do accept receive our personal, careful attention. For example, we take the time to meet with your doctors and discuss with them how they can assist in your case. I recently met with a client's doctor and discovered information that was not in the medical records – that information added $65,000 in value to her case! A high-volume practice that does not take the time to carefully review your medical documents, meet with medical providers, and develop a legal strategy specifically tailored to the circumstances of each case would have missed this and settled the case for much less than its true value.

Cases We Do Not Accept

We have found that the only way to provide personal service is to decline those cases that do not meet our strict criteria. Therefore, at Christensen & Hymas, we generally do not accept the following types of cases:

- Cases involving minor impact or no visible damage to the vehicle. Our experience with juries is that by and large, they do not believe a minor impact could cause substantial personal injury, even when well-qualified experts testify otherwise. As a result, these cases often result in very low verdicts. Thus, we believe that the risk to the client is too great to warrant pursuing these claims. There are other attorneys with different opinions about these types of cases and, if you call my office, I will be happy to provide you with recommendations for such attorneys.
- Cases with less than $3,500 of expected medical bills. Your case must have at least $3,500 in past and future medical bills before we will consider accepting it. We would like to represent everyone who needs a good attorney, but we cannot. Remember, we are talking about your total medical bills, not just your "out-of-pocket" expenses, which may be less. If you have a question about this, contact us and we can help you figure it out.
- Cases where you have a significant pre-existing injury in the same area of the body. If you have had numerous surgeries or treatments for your low back, and your low back is later injured in an accident, our experience shows that juries will not award you much compensation for that injury. In our opinion, the time and risk associated with these cases is simply too great to pursue, unless your doctor can clearly distinguish which injuries were caused by the accident, and which were pre-existing.

- Cases where you were found to be at fault by the police officer. We will not represent you if you were charged or cited by the police officer for causing the accident. I understand that police officers make mistakes and that you may disagree or believe the police officer was wrong, but we are unwilling to represent you in these instances.
- Cases where you were found to be mostly at fault by the police. Even if the other driver shares some blame, we are unwilling to represent someone who was deemed to be primarily at fault for the accident. However, if the other driver bears most of the fault, we may be able to help, depending on other facts involved in your case. Feel free to contact us to discuss the circumstances of your case free of charge.
- If you have had several serious accident claims in the near past, we will not accept your case. We have found that jurors tend to look unfavorably on claimants who have a significant accident history.
- Cases where you have a significant and prior criminal record involving fraud, deceit or dishonesty. The credibility of the injured person is one of the most important aspects of a personal injury claim. As a result, clients who have a criminal history (particularly one that involves dishonesty, fraud or deceit) are viewed with a great degree of skepticism by jurors.
- Cases that are near the end of the statute of limitations. We generally like to have at least four months to evaluate and investigate your claim. This is another reason why you should not delay in contacting an attorney.

- Cases where you currently have an attorney who has represented you for more than three months. If an attorney already represents you, this book can increase your knowledge and help you ask proper questions about your case. It is often too late for us to pursue the case in the manner that we believe is best for you.

Well, Are There Any Cases Left?

Yes, there are, and that's just the point. As I said before, our office represents many good people with valid claims. We have found that we do our best work by devoting our time and resources to cases that meet our criteria, rather than getting bogged down in claims riddled with many of the problems and challenges identified above. That is why we have made the decision to keep our caseload small, and concentrate our efforts on creating lasting relationships with clients and working together to obtain the best results for our clients.

What Do Our Past Clients Have To Say?

Here is a sampling of what our past clients have to say. There are others at our website at www.utahpersonalinjurylawfirm.com.

"I am so grateful Ken Christensen was recommended to me. The part that amazed me most was his personal service. I never had to wait for him to respond; anytime I called, he either talked to me right then or called back within minutes. With every problem that came up, he jumped right on it, even if it was something he wasn't obligated to do. In a bad situation, Ken made things a lot easier to deal with and was very thorough in explaining the entire process to me. I would have been lost without him. He did a spectacular job!!"

Amy Kerbs, South Jordan, UT

"I am writing this letter to give my unqualified endorsement of Ken Christensen and his firm. In January of 2007 I was rear-ended by a drunk driver while stopped at a red light. During the accident I sustained injuries to my neck, back, and shoulder. A good friend of mine suggested I call Ken. I am so glad I did. Ken took over everything from dealing with the police and insurance companies to working with my health care providers to ensure they were paid. I never had to deal with my insurance company or the other driver's insurance company. Christensen & Hymas also handled any billing issues from my many health care providers.

All my medical bills were paid in full, and my claim was settled at the maximum benefit allowed by the other driver's insurance plan. I have absolutely no reservation in recommending Ken Christensen and his firm. In fact, I have recommended them to family and friends. If you are in the need of effective and ethical representation, I strongly recommend that you call Christensen & Hymas."

Eric C. Evans, Draper, UT

"I am very skeptical of lawyers. I was taken advantage of by a firm in Nebraska and swore I would not use another attorney again. My own insurance company made it so difficult, so I finally called these guys when I saw the ad on TV. Best decision I made! I highly recommend this firm. Their book is full of useful knowledge. Everyone should read it before they are in an accident. I never could have done this without them. It was overwhelming with the bills and insurance companies and adjusters and not knowing if they were looking out for me. Christensen & Hymas took care of everything and made sure I didn't make a mistake. I got a great settlement that I don't think I could have received on my own and didn't have to worry about anything. They followed up on all the details, including my health insurance, and took the stress away."

Anne Hart, Riverton, UT

"I was in an automobile accident last July where a man ran a red light and hit my vehicle. I received various injuries that required numerous procedures and office visits. Being an avid runner, I was so concerned about my long term physical disabilities. Trying to work with the different insurance companies was very difficult until I hired Christensen & Hymas. I so appreciated their professionalism and the fact that they really care about their clients. I will always be grateful for their assistance and compassion."

Merilyn Haslam, Ogden, UT

"I came to Christensen & Hymas with two different cases. I first heard about the law firm through a friend. When I came into the office, everyone was very friendly. It was attorney Russ Hymas who was working on my cases. I was always comfortable talking with Russ. Russ always greeted me with a smile, and I never had any issues talking to him about my cases. If he was not in, there were always friendly people working in the office that would assure that my needs were always taken care of. I would highly recommend Christensen & Hymas."

Misty McGuire, West Jordan, UT

"My husband and I were devastated and confused as our teenage daughter lay in a coma after a terrible accident. An already emotional situation was made worse by insurance companies and attorneys that seemed so insensitive to our situation. That's why it's hard for me to express how grateful we were to have

Ken and Russ on our side. We really appreciated the way they stood up for our family. They made multiple trips to the hospital, contacted medical providers, and helped with her funeral expenses after her passing. I really appreciate the assistance they provided during an overwhelming time."

Rebecca Ewell, Magna, UT

"Working with the insurance companies before we hired Christensen & Hymas was very confusing. I kept getting pushed around, and no one could ever give me a straight answer. This all changed after we met with Ken Christensen and hired his firm. They handled everything, so I could focus on healing. They exceeded my expectations! They were extremely helpful and knowledgeable, and called me with monthly updates on the status of my case."

Koryanne Freeze, Brigham City, UT

"I knew that I needed an attorney after my accident, but I hesitated approaching one—I'm not the type of person who sues for anything and everything. That's why I'm so glad I contacted Christensen & Hymas. They obtained a great settlement for me, without even having to file a lawsuit against the driver who hit me. I was impressed by the quick responses and professionalism shown by everyone at the firm. My experience was much better than I had ever anticipated."

Jason Haddock, Sandy, UT

GLOSSARY

Bodily Injury
Any bodily injury, sickness, disease or death sustained by any person

Insured
A person covered under an insurance policy. This can be the actual person paying for the insurance policy, immediate family members, occupants of the vehicle, and any other person using the vehicle within the scope of your permission

Medical Expenses
Usual, customary and reasonable expenses for necessary medical, surgical, x-ray, ambulance, hospital, professional nursing, funerals, and dental services, including prosthetic devices

Personal Injury Protection (PIP)
Also known as "no-fault coverage." Allows for at least $3,000 for reasonable and necessary medical expenses, the lesser of $250 per week or 85% of any loss of gross income, lost household services to be paid at $20.00 per day for a maximum of one year, $1,500 for funeral expenses, and death benefits payable to the heirs in the amount of $3,000

Policy Limits
The maximum amount available for claims based on the coverage contracted for under the insurance policy

Property Damage
Physical injury to or destruction of tangible property, including the loss of use of such property

Subrogation
A reimbursement claim by a third party (typically a health insurance company) that is made against the settlement proceeds

Underinsured Motorist Coverage (UIM)
Coverage available under your personal automobile insurance policy when the at-fault driver's insurance policy has been exhausted but is insufficient to fully cover the injuries and damages

Uninsured Motorist Coverage (UM)
Coverage available under your personal automobile insurance policy for an accident with a vehicle that does not have insurance or an accident with an unidentified hit-and-run vehicle

DIRECTIONS TO OUR OFFICES

Directions to Our Draper Office

Christensen Building
11693 South 700 East, Suite 100
Draper, UT 84020
(801) 506-0800

From the North: Take Exit 292/11400 South on the I-15 Freeway and go east. Turn south on 700 East. You will see our red two-story brick building on the left.

From the South: Take Exit 291/12300 South on the I-15 Freeway and go east. Turn north on 700 East. Once you pass Kimballs Lane, our red two-story brick building will be on the right side of the road.

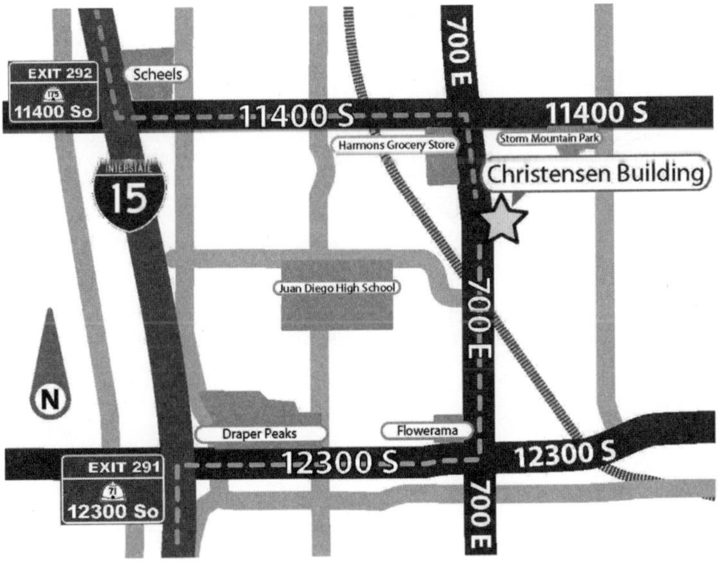

Directions to Our Bountiful Office

Take Exit 315/2600 South on the I-15 Freeway and travel east to the Square Shopping Center near 500 West on the south side of the road. Our office is in the northeast corner of the shopping center in a large gray building next to Costa Vida Restaurant. Our office is upstairs.

By Appointment Only
503 West 2600 South
Bountiful, Utah 84010
(801) 294-9500

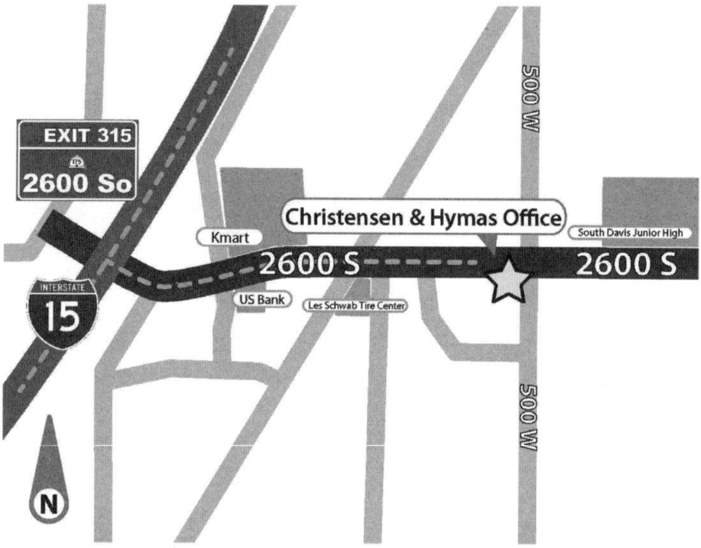

Directions to Our Orem Office

From the North: Take Exit 271/Center St on the I-15 Freeway and travel east on Center St. Turn south onto State Street. Our office is located in the Troon Business Park, kitty corner to the Scera Pool.

From the South: Take Exit 269/University Parkway and travel east on University Parkway. Turn north onto State Street. Our office is located in the Troon Business Park, kitty-corner to the Scera Pool.

By Appointment Only
574 South State St.
Orem, UT 84058
(801) 224-2999

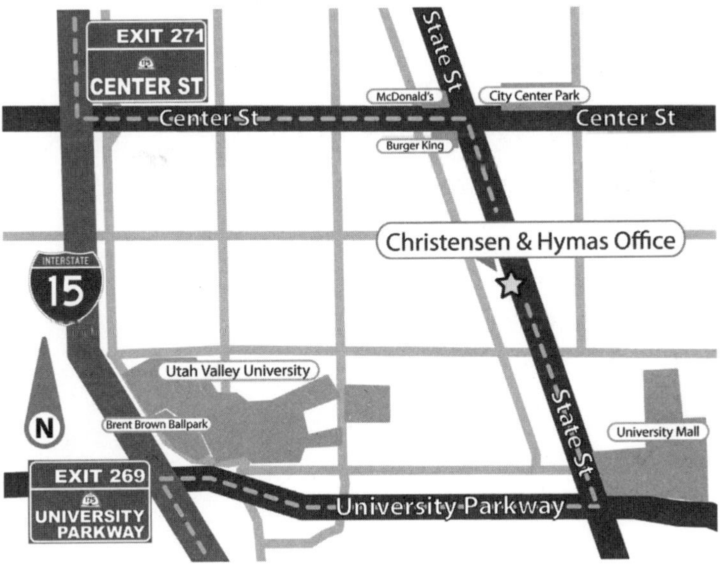